HELL FIRE
IS REAL

HELL FIRE IS REAL

MY EXPERIENCE

AUTHOR:

HOPE STEWART

WRITTEN BY:

TANYA FREW

Author/writer of Utmost Love: Dark & Light-shade Emotions

Rev. date: 09/10/2020

To order additional copies of this book, contact:
Xlibris
UK TFN: 0800 0148620 (Toll Free inside the UK)
UK Local: 02036 956328 (+44 20 3695 6328 from outside the UK)
www.Xlibrispublishing.co.uk
Orders@Xlibrispublishing.co.uk
818477

Thank you, Tanya Frew (author and writer), for developing my story and writing it! You made this book possible and have literally turned my dream into reality.

This book is NOT about religion! It is about serving Jesus Christ, and reaping the spiritual reward—heaven.

HELLFIRE IS VERY REAL . . .

God created us in the likeness of His image. No one was created for hell, but hell was created for those who choose Satan's kingdom.

For my son and all the people who have supported me throughout . . .

ACKNOWLEDGEMENT

Sincere thanks to Mojarie Kennedy, who
encouraged me to write this book.

PREFACE

Talking about hell is a ridiculously hot topic, and it is most times too hot to touch on. Many people, especially non-believers, are only too happy to shut you down. Why would anyone talk about hell? It is a worst-case scenario, if it exists at all, or so they may be thinking. Everyone will eventually die and go to heaven, they say, even if they do not believe there is a God! How could one believe in heaven, but does not believe there is a hell? If every coin has two sides, then surely hell is on the flip side of heaven.

This story is about to enlighten us how real hell is. I hope there are others who can relate . . .

INTRODUCTION

This story is based on my own experiences. It is not one I feel should be taken lightly, and it is nothing short of incredible! I am unable to hold back, as this was not an everyday occurrence. My experiences had left me shivering to my bones like nothing else could . . .

If I did not believe that Jesus Christ is the son of Jehovah Jireh, and they are a part of the Holy Trinity (Father, Son, and the Holy Spirit), then I do believe now. I would like to share with the world that God is real! And He will be coming back to secure His chosen ones. Everyone needs to get ready to meet our king. The words of the Bible are true. Open your eyes and see, before one day, you will hear, 'Depart from me, I know you not.'

CONTENTS

CHAPTER 1

HELL IS REAL

Beliefs are based on upbringing, culture, and experiences. Some people believe in Jehovah Jireh. Others believe in various types of gods, idols, or nothing at all. Whilst I struggle to see proof of other gods existing, it is hard to ignore the fulfilment of the Bible. For instance, Matthew 24:6–14 highlights there will be wars and rumours of wars; nations will be rising up against nations and kingdoms against kingdoms. There will be famine, pestilences, and earthquakes in diverse places—all these things are the beginning of sorrow. Those who adhere to God's words will be hated for His name's sake. And because of the overwhelming abundance of hatred, people's hearts will become waxed cold—no love. But the children of God who endure to the end will be saved. Once the gospel is preached in all the world, the end will be. I think it is fair to say, we are already seeing these things today without stating all the humanitarian and political uprisings around the world.

God wants everyone to have an understanding of His words, and will not leave anyone out. His warnings are clear, and we should give ear to these words.

Matthew 24:2

And Jesus said unto them, see ye not all these things? Verily I say unto you, there shall not be left here one stone upon another, that shall not be thrown down.

From observation, it is clear many people are yet to accept Jesus Christ. We seem to appreciate just about everything else, except the truth. I just want to say, God is real, and waiting for **all** to acknowledge the reality of heaven and hell.

Are we blinded by worldly phenomena?

Are we afraid of committing to holiness?

What is holding us back?

Will we embrace hell or heaven?

For those who do not believe hell exists, there is a place called hell! Hell is very real. This is where people who do not live according to Jehovah's laws will spend eternity. I am no exception. If I do not live for God, I will miss my place in heaven. Back in the day, JUDGEMENT DAY used to be frequently mentioned. But these days, everything is diluted or obsolete to those who want to blotch out aspects of our spiritual reality. Hiding away from biblical facts will not make judgement day any easier. God's laws are already in place and timely fulfilling. Therefore, nothing will be changed to suit mankind. Maybe it is time we change something, or a lot of things. Change requires sacrifice, but are we willing to make such a sacrifice for our own sakes? Making godly sacrifices now would be the most important thing we could ever do.

REFLECTION

Be open to understanding Jehovah
Know that God is for us, not against us
Positive changes are rewarding
Motivate your thoughts in an upward direction
Understand the value of sacrifices

CHAPTER

MY EXPERIENCE

I was transported to hell, twice in two years. This happened whilst I was sleeping—in a dream. It seems, there was no night or day—it was 'hell time'! The land was filled with misery. I could see souls in hell, tormented and burning eternally. The fire was so real—it was like a million jumbo jets crashed into one place. The scene was just incredible, beyond anyone's natural imagination! People had nowhere else to go, but hell. Everyone was in the same position, whilst there were weeping and wailing. Quite interestingly, I did not see mansions, cars, designer clothes, banks, millionaires, or billionaires—just people and their burning flesh. I have never seen such a sad sight, ever! How horrifying and scary it was. It was heart-rending to virtually experience.

When I think of the intensity and magnitude of hell, my heart sank immensely. I felt as if everything inside me fell through and hit the ground—my body sensed hollowness. I struggled to comprehend, and have brought myself to a serene place to process it all. On reflection, I realised that my purpose at the scene was to watch as a messenger. God wants me to share what He does not want to happen to us. Therefore, God wants us to acknowledge His greatness now; that He may not disown us in the end.

Revelation 20:15

And whosoever was not found in the book of life was cast into the lake of fire.

God expects people to ascertain purity, and not evil. Blessed are those with pure hearts, for they shall see God (Matt. 5:8). The works of the unjust will not go unpunished.

Revelation 2:8

But the fearful, and unbelieving, and the abominable, and murderers, and whoremongers, and sorcerers, and idolaters, and all liars, shall have their part in the lake which burneth with fire and brimstone: which is the second death.

Once there is life, there is hope—as the old saying goes. So there is time for us to seek God! This is our time to get our lives on the straight and narrow path. There is one thing I am certain of: there is no repentance in the grave. God's words do not fall and vanished. They will all come to pass. Jesus firmly ascertained in Matthew 24:34, this generation will not pass until all things ordained are being fulfilled.

Matthew 24:35

Heaven and earth shall pass away, but my words shall never pass away.

No one knows the day when God will return (Matt. 24:36), but His return is certain. So let today count by means of spiritual reflection and awareness.

Acts 17:30–31

And the time of this ignorance God winketh at; but now commandeth all men everywhere to repent. Because he

hath appointed a day, in which he will judge the world in righteousness . . .

Luke 24:47

And that repentance and remission of sins should be preached in his name among all nations, beginning at Jerusalem.

Which side are you on—the righteous or unrighteous?

Hell is not an option for the righteous and committed Christians, as that is the sole purpose of being devoted children of God. Nevertheless, there are people who know about God and what He stands for. They even profess Christianity and inwardly desire to live righteously, but struggle to do so. And then, there are others who have a vague knowledge or do not know about God. But Jehovah has a mission to solve this variance *(see later chapters)*. Because in His eyes, people are either righteous or unrighteous. It is therefore imperative for people to not be overshadowed by spiritual ignorance. Make the effort to reinforce godliness and truth. Surely, God does not force anyone to choose Him. But where there is no choice, the unrighteous lose their birthright—such consequential price to pay! Why should we suffer, when we have a holy and forgiving Father in heaven who does not want us to perish? Christ is not partial towards His people. It does not matter who you are or what you have done to an extent, Christ's arms are wide-stretched open, ready to embrace and forgive. He forgives all sins, except blasphemy.

Acts 29:18

To open their eyes, and to turn them from darkness to light, and from the power of Satan unto God, that they may receive forgiveness of sins, and inheritance among them which are sanctified by faith that is in me.

Mark 3:28–29

Verily I say unto you, all sins shall be forgiven unto the sons of men, and blasphemies wherewith soever they shall blaspheme:

But he that shall blaspheme against the Holy Ghost hath never forgiveness, but is in danger of eternal damnation.

What more should we expect or ask of God?

God gave us a beautiful earth to enjoy, filled with all we need to strive happily. Can we find it in us to serve Him the way He deserves to be served? And indeed, give us a chance of eternal life in heaven?

God Forgives

Forgive yourself, and do not hold back,
As our Father in heaven, hath forgiven you,
And on His words, He does not go back.
Accept His mercies and grace,
Knowing, our heavenly home He has prepared,
And it is a very safe place.
End eternal pain, before it begins,
Thus, take on the coat of righteousness,
And bury all your sins.
Just live for Christ Jesus,
In peace and harmony, not deceits and fuss.
That you may miss hell,
And nothing more to tell.

REFLECTION

Understand the significance of visions
Acknowledge God's purpose for His creation
Evaluate your spiritual status with
God: are you righteous?
Repentance is a spiritual filtration
Is God's forgiving nature enough for you?
Choose your master
Where is your destination, heaven or hell?

CHAPTER

WAKE UP . . .

There are many sleeping churches. By this, I mean Christians who are unable to see their spiritual pathway because they are walking with their mind-eyes closed. Lacking visions of their own, they missed out on seeing where God wants them to be and what He wants them to do. Therefore, they rely on others to lead them entirely—unknown to them whether they are on the right path or not. In some cases, leaders who are recognised as pastors and bishops are walking by sight and not by **faith;** hence, their lack spiritual direction. This, therefore, reflects 'the blind leading the blind' scenario.

Are we awake or in a slumber mode?

Fundamentally, people need to live by faith or they will slumber. Faith is the key to opening Christians' pathways. Without faith, there can be no true direction. It means, when you seek directions, your faith runs miles ahead to create your path, and make possible what you have asked for. But of course, unless you understand the spiritual context of faith, you will struggle to have clear visions. Always project your faith upward and forward to benefit; believe sincerely through prayer. God designed faith to aid choices. Stay awake and let your chosen path be framed by faith.

Have faith like a flowing river—show direction and purpose! Propel your faith with constant prayer and positivity. Be the epitome of your spiritual intentions. When you live and breathe faith, leaders cannot easily mislead you! Because if they deviate from the path of righteousness, your faith and vision will keep you focused on your destiny.

Hebrews 11:1

Now, faith is the substance of things hoped for, the evidence of things not seen.

Choose wisely

Leaders are not entirely responsible for Christians' lives, but here only to offer guidance. However, people of God need to choose their leaders carefully, with eyes and minds wide open. Not all leaders are of God, some are pretentious false prophets. They exhibit similar attributes to godly leaders, although they are working directly with the devil.

Matthew 7:15

Beware of false prophets, which come to you in sheep's clothing, but inwardly they are ravening wolves.

Matthew 24:5

For many shall come in my name, saying, I am Christ; and shall deceive many.

People of God, if you are in slumber mode—wake up!

Leaders of God, if you are driving the spiritual train, but it is on autopilot—wake up!

Christians, if you are not sure of your destination—wake up!

People of the world, if you have not chosen your holy path yet—wake up!

Children of God, it is time we check which road we are on. Broad is the road, which leads to destruction; narrow is the road, which leads to heaven. Do not get to your destination, only to realise you are at hell's gate! It will be too late, as there will be no turning back. Come on, wake up and get ready for the kingdom of God!

Matthew 7:21

Not everyone who says Lord, Lord, shall enter the kingdom of heaven, but he who does the will of my Father in heaven.

A business for God's kingdom?

Christians most obvious mission is to strive for the kingdom of God. And we must do this according to instructions written in the Bible. However, in many instances, some of these instructions are now diluted to suit our personal lives. For instance, I do not understand why some churches are named after head pastors or bishops, instead of biblical names that are associated with God. I can understand if pastors' homes have their names written over their front doors—that is personal! Should this shift be acceptable? Whenever there are shifts in churches, I can see pastors and bishops shifting too. They often move so far away from God; their institutions do not represent what God stands for anymore. It becomes more about their own personal missions—God's business is now secondary, and is only mentioned to pull people into their 'supposedly godly house'. This is not in all cases, I might add.

Do leaders still preach holiness?

These days, the messages preached in churches are so different from what we would normally hear. It is less about righteousness, the kingdom of God that is at hand, love your neighbours as thyself as taught by Jesus Christ, but is much more about worldly attainment—money and power. For those who can afford to be flashy, they do not hesitate to compete, showing off their best car, flashiest suits, and biggest houses. At times, Christians are so caught up with their desires, they have forgotten time is going by, and God is coming back again for a holy church. A church that represents the body of Christ.

Repent, repent, repent, repent, repent, the kingdom of God is at hand! These are the most repetitive words leaders in the past would preach. It was so important that people would repent daily, if not hourly. No one wanted to miss heaven. Hence, it was imperative to strip back spiritually. Clean hands and a pure heart shall see God.

Are great leaders still about?

Leaders are often held in high esteem, regardless of whether they are prophets, shepherds, pastors, bishops, or any other title. However, God does not inspire great leaders based on their literal intellects. God expects leaders to put aside self, ego, pride, prejudice, and arrogance; and humbly seek wisdom, knowledge, and understanding. God wants leaders to girdle themselves in His love and be equipped with the word of God, and know His laws and premise. Exemplary leaders who are like Moses, Noah, Joseph, and Joshua, exhibit Christlike leadership qualities, in ways that are pleasing to God! These leaders showed strength, courage, embraced holiness, battleship, ruled fairly, and served continuously. Christian leaders should first come to God humbly like children, ready to listen to His perfect guidance on their leads. Great leaders aspire to protect and guide people towards the light—away from darkness through the manifestation of God's will . . .

It is always such a delight to acknowledge leaders whose work exhibits spiritual proficiency. Those who know the importance of valuing their positions as leaders and show appreciation for the trust Christians put in them.

Leaders, offerings, and tithes

God is kind and generous—and this is how He wants us to be towards each other. God wants us to accept and acknowledge the importance of sharing. This is always especially for the benefit of others. However, I do not believe God wants people to be stripped of their finances for the benefit of those who are eagerly after overnight wealth. In many churches, leaders are prone to constantly collect money, in the name of tithes and offering, followed by preaching about the significance of paying up. And as if this is not enough, they would promote moneymaking programmes, which are only beneficial to them. Whilst they covertly share the money among themselves, some church members are starving.

Not everyone can afford to pay up in church, on the demands of church leaders. There are Christians who do not earn enough money, or even earn at all. And sometimes leaders are not being sensitive to everyone's situation. I believe there should be no pressure to give out money in the house of God. Members should give towards the maintenance of the church, share and care in honest ways—if they can afford to. Also, everyone should have the right to know how money collected is spent.

My experience

A few years ago, I attended a church where they gave out white envelopes and told us, the Lord said everyone ought to give £31. But I knew for sure that was not from God, as I did not even have £5. God would never ask you to give what you do not have.

. . . Another occasion

There was a time when I financially supported a church ministry by giving £30 a month. However, it so happened, I was not working for quite some time. One day, I got a phone call from the church officer asking why I did not send in my money. I told her I was not working, and I do not have any money. And instead of asking how I was managing, she said, 'How can you be a Christian and do not have money?' I explained that I was sick and not working. Also, I am uncertain when I will return to work. And guess what? She just hung up the phone. Quite interestingly, when church members are struggling financially, the leaders are more likely to say, let me pray that God will open doors for you. But they will not open doors for you by dipping hands in their pockets and offer even £1.

Someone's testimony

I was once invited to a church in London where I listened to a member's testimony. She had lost her job that week, and her rent was due the following week. She had no idea, how she was going to manage, and her daughter had to go to school. After she finished speaking, she went back to her seat and sat down. The bishop got up and spoke to the church, he suggested no one should tell this lady to pray that God will provide. He then asked the congregation to put money together for her—he had made the first offer, and everyone else followed. The lady gracefully accepted.

A week later, the lady gave another testimony. On this occasion, she had found another job, paid her expenses, and life was as it should be again. She spoke for a few minutes, and went on to say, it was her fault why she had lost her job. And this bishop was the only minister whom she knew did such kind gesture. So maybe there are charitable leaders out there. But perhaps I do not personally know any. However, it goes to show **when** Christians are living for God, we can relate to the world in special ways. One for all and all for—and not all for one, whilst one is only for himself or herself.

Money vs. God

Money is temporary, and so is its value. It can buy many things, except for health and salvation. God created all things, including giving mankind the intelligence and ability to create money. But God does not like greed, as demonstrated in Luke.

Luke 12:15

And he said unto them, take heed, and beware of covetousness: for a man's life consisteth not in the abundance of the things which he possesseth.

Arise and shine

Daughters and sons of God, arise, shine, and give God the glory! Let us make the works of God our primary focus—serve God, give love, care, and support.

Missionaries

When was the last time pastors randomly visited prisoners?

When was the last time we gave away some of our designer clothes or any aid to the homeless?

When was the last time we gave food to those who are starving?

When was the last time we helped a vulnerable person?

When was the last time we visited our elderly neighbours?

People of God, let us get our acts together.

Matthew 25:43

I was a stranger and you did not invite me in, I needed clothes, and you did not clothe me, I was sick and in prison and you did not look after me.

REFLECTION

Have strong faith
Let faith frame our world
Faith shows evidence of what is real
Visions are impossible without faith

Spiritual pathways are visible with faith
Faith propels godliness and good works
Faith is intangible and always ahead of you
There is power in words

CHAPTER

CHILDREN OF GOD OR AGENTS OF SATAN?

Many years ago, in the 1970s, I was a young member of a church. And in a dream, the Lord showed me the ministers naked with their genitals exposed, whilst celebrating with bottles of rums and whiskies. I unwittingly told the bishop my dream. He told me the dream was not from God. 'Come, let me pray for you, that the Lord will show you good dreams.' He puts his hand on my head and prayed God will let me have good dreams. From that day on, the dreams I used to have were no more. Eventually, I went back and told him, 'I do not dream those dreams anymore.' He prayed for me again, that I will have good dreams. However, I was not feeling comfortable with his presence, and I did not understand why. Nevertheless, I soon realised that the bishop and his pastors were involved in witchcraft, but I did not quite understand the level of witchcraft in the church. A few weeks later, that bishop had a stroke. He had sent me messages and requested, I come and visit him. But by then, I had met a new pastor who listened to my story and advised me not to see him. So I did not return.

The sex-addicted pastors

My heart grieves to acknowledge that some pastors would have the audacity to ask church members for sex. Should they be asking anyone for sex, except their lawful partners? Leaders, who should be living holy for God, nurture their addiction without taking those affected into consideration, or even their Christian status. A stranger once shared with me her disgust when her pastor asked for them to sleep together. But even more confusing for her, he had continued ministering in their church.

Disgusting, right?

My experience in this respect is not quite as bad, but it was still unacceptable when I saw a pastor watching pornography on his laptop at church.

Vigilant Christians

People of God ought to be careful of those who are leading. Know your leaders—be sure they are shepherds and not wolves in suits. Do not follow leaders because you think it is right, or it is what others expect of you. Do it because you believe in their exemplary lives. Also, do it because you are confident your leaders are guiding you to the path of righteousness. Do not always accept what other people know as your truth, but equip yourself with the word of God, and find your own truth.

REFLECTION

Be careful who is laying hands on you
Who is your leader's master?
Look out for unfaithful leaders
Trust God to fill your basket when it is empty

CHAPTER

BETTER IN THAN OUT

In general, people have uncountable questions about God—and rightly so! There is much to know about God. However, we need to make time to read, pray, and listen to God in order to have such knowledge. God is a mysterious spirit who connects with us through our inner spirit. But there is nothing we need to know that He has not already made clear to us (*read the Bible*). We exist because of God. Jehovah created us to be His vessels—perfect partnership, Holy Spirit and vessels, right? So it is fair to say, God needs us too. He wants us to trust Him explicitly, to the point where we take no thought of ourselves—as that is His job! So yes, proclaimers of God, our sole purpose is to serve God! And if we are not doing God's will, then we are a not preparing ourselves for what is to come.

God warns about a series of events which are to come leading to judgement—the end of all things bad and the beginning of all things glorious! Judgement will take place over a period. Even though some people may be under the assumption, it will be one day (*read the book of Revelation*). It will not be! Some of these events include fulfilling the mission of the church, the appearance of the throne of God, the uprising of the beasts, the great red dragon with seven heads and ten horns, the bottomless pit, vial of wrath to be poured upon the earth, bounding of Satan's freedom for a thousand years, a new heaven and a new earth. Yes, a new heaven and a new earth, for those who righteously proclaim His words.

It would be perfectly amazing for God if everyone would fulfil their purpose. However, God knows many will be unfaithful, like Judas, and betray Him. But God has a plan to reward the just and the unjust, according to their works.

Revelation 22:12

And, behold I come quickly; and my reward is with me, to give every man according to his work shall be.

Not everyone gives hearing to God's words, some are literally deaf; and of those who can hear, many will not listen. But God said, let those who hear and listen, what the spirit said unto the churches, overcome and eat from the tree of life, which is in the midst of God's paradise (Rev. 2:7).

Believe it or not, there are Christians who do not always hear God's voice, because there is too much chaos—no peace! On the other hand, Christians also have moments when they recognised God is speaking to them, though unable to act upon His instructions because fear, anger, intellect, and stress are in operation—causing interference and doubts. Therefore, it is important to zone-out of your literal being and allow your spirit to connect with God in order to listen and hear effectively. The voice of God is still, and requires quietness and attentiveness for us to hear.

Revelation 22:16

I Jesus have sent mine angel to testify unto you these things in the churches. I am the root and the offspring of David, and the bright and morning star.

God stays true to His unchangeable words; so we are reminded, His promises are real. Be not ashamed of God. Praise Him in great adoration.

Revelation 22:21

The grace of the Lord Jesus Christ be with you all. Amen.

REFLECTION

Put God first
Are you a proclaimer?
Better to be in heaven than hell
Connect your spirit with God by denying self
The book of Revelation—the end time
We belong to God

CHAPTER

THE BOTTOMLESS PIT

In my dream, when God transported me to hell (chapter 2), I saw the bottomless pit. The extraordinary fire was red and orange. When the blaze was raging, I could see souls walking into the bottomless pit of fire. There were so many people in hell—countless, like a colony of ants. I saw some famous and familiar faces entering Satan's kingdom. But there were times the fire was low and clouds of smoke filled the air—it was pitch-black! I could not see anyone anymore.

Hell is real!

The book of Revelation highlights the entire journey to heaven and hell. It is very eye-opening and perceptively dark in many parts. And for this reason, I can understand why some people are fearful of this book. But, as ignorance is not bliss, I made it my job to read. I would encourage everyone to read through Revelation at least once in their lifetime, although it would be even better for us to educate ourselves biblically by reading the entire Bible.

Revelation chapter 9 highlights the purpose of the bottomless pit.

Revelation 9

¹ And the fifth angel sounded, and I saw a star fall from heaven unto the earth: and to him was given the key of the bottomless pit.

² And he opened the bottomless pit; and there arose a smoke out of the pit, as the smoke of a great furnace; and the sun and the air were darkened by reason of the smoke of the pit.

³ And there came out of the smoke locusts upon the earth: and unto them was given power, as the scorpions of the earth have power.

⁴ And it was commanded them that they should not hurt the grass of the earth, neither any green thing, neither any tree; but only those men which have not the seal of God in their foreheads.

⁵ And to them it was given that they should not kill them, but that they should be tormented five months: and their torment was as the torment of a scorpion, when he striketh a man.

⁶ And in those days shall men seek death, and shall not find it; and shall desire to die, and death shall flee from them.

⁷ And the shapes of the locusts were like unto horses prepared unto battle; and on their heads were as it were crowns like gold, and their faces were as the faces of men.

⁸ And they had hair as the hair of women, and their teeth were as the teeth of lions.

⁹ And they had breastplates, as it were breastplates of iron; and the sound of their wings was as the sound of chariots of many horses running to battle.

¹⁰ And they had tails like unto scorpions, and there were stings in their tails: and their power was to hurt men five months.

¹¹ And they had a king over them, which is the angel of the bottomless pit, whose name in the Hebrew tongue is Abaddon, but in the Greek tongue hath his name Apollyon.

¹² One woe is past; and, behold, there come two woes more hereafter.

¹³ And the sixth angel sounded, and I heard a voice from the four horns of the golden altar which is before God,

¹⁴ Saying to the sixth angel which had the trumpet, Loose the four angels which are bound in the great river Euphrates.

¹⁵ And the four angels were loosed, which were prepared for an hour, and a day, and a month, and a year, for to slay the third part of men.

¹⁶ And the number of the army of the horsemen were two hundred thousand thousand: and I heard the number of them.

¹⁷ And thus I saw the horses in the vision, and them that sat on them, having breastplates of fire, and of jacinth, and brimstone: and the heads of the horses were as the heads of lions; and out of their mouths issued fire and smoke and brimstone.

¹⁸ By these three was the third part of men killed, by the fire, and by the smoke, and by the brimstone, which issued out of their mouths.

¹⁹ For their power is in their mouth, and in their tails: for their tails were like unto serpents, and had heads, and with them they do hurt.

²⁰ And the rest of the men which were not killed by these plagues yet repented not of the works of their hands, that they should not worship devils, and idols of gold, and silver, and brass, and stone, and of wood: which neither can see, nor hear, nor walk:

[21] Neither repented they of their murders, nor of their sorceries, nor of their fornication, nor of their thefts.

REFLECTION

Is the bottomless pit for you?

Recognise the importance of serving God

Be guided by the Bible

CHAPTER

POWER OF PRAYER

To effectively connect with God through prayer, it is crucial to pray in solitude. It is like having an intimate time with someone you love—yes, intimate, close and personal, not sexual! And in those moments, you give your undivided attention and relax your mind and body. Bring yourself to a place, where you feel accepted and content in God's presence. And when you are ready to utter what is on your mind, then God is already there with you, listening and ready to speak to your inner spirit. Remember, this is a spirit-to-spirit connection. A time to immerse in divinity, and forget about the earthly things which cloud your mind.

Matthew 6:6

But thou, when thou prayest, enter into thy closet, and when thou hast shut thy door, pray to thy Father which is in secret; and thy Father which seeth in secret shall reward thee openly.

Jesus taught us to pray; He prayed to the Father (Matt. 6:9–13).

Our Father which art in heaven,
Hallowed be thy name.
Thy kingdom come,

Thy will be done in earth,
As it is in heaven.
Give us this day our daily bread.
And forgive us our debts,
as we forgive our debtors.
And lead us not into temptation,
But deliver us from evil:
For thine is the kingdom,
The power, and the glory,
Amen.

So now we know who we pray to. Let us create a daily prayer routine and become prayer warriors for God. Jehovah appreciates warriors, although He does not expect us to pray the same way. What you say in prayer, how and when you pray, is up to you as prayers usually reflect experiences, emotions, and definitely personality. David had prayed uncountable prayers, and they varied (book of Psalms).

Making time for prayer is important! Prayer should not be a chore but rather a high priority. Prayer time can be long or short—God accepts them all. Pray when you are well and happy. Pray when you are ill, upset, and filled with worry—especially then, you should be pressing to pray. Pray when you do not feel there is a reason to pray—as there is always something or someone to be prayed for. Prayer can be in the form of worship: giving God praises and also spiritual cleansing.

Did you know, prayer is powerful? It sure is . . .

Cementing your relationship with God through prayer is a good way to experience the power of prayer. Faith and prayer walk together; it is impossible to experience the power of prayer without faith. You got to believe in who you are praying to, what your prayer is about, and your outcome expectancy. If anyone prays and asks God for wisdom, he shall receive liberally (James 1:5). But he must ask in faith, without waver—for anyone who wavers, is like the waves of the sea, driven by the wind and tossed (James 1: 6).

Mark 11:24

Therefore I say unto you, what things soever ye desire, when ye pray, believe that ye receive them, and ye shall receive them.

Be patient—wait on God!

When we pray, we must wait—wait on God to respond. God does not work with our timing, but His own—which is not always in accordance with our desires. We like things done now . . . and results straight away! But God works with time and patience. Yes, pray and wait for God to give the right answer and best outcomes. Because we have a good relationship with God, it does not mean He sings to our every tune. God does not necessarily supply our wants, but our needs. God delivers on His own terms! After all, He is the master, not us. God knows best, we have to trust Him!

Humble Prayer

Wonderful God, I have sinned uncountable times,
And my faults are unlimited,
But I am glad you are still standing by me,
Being consistent and divine.
I know my lifestyle does not represent you,
And I hope to change it,
So please forgive me of my sins,
And once more, make me feel brand new.
Open my mind, and let me see,
The things which are pure,
And let holiness resides in me.
Keep me grounded, humble and true,
No backbiting, and falseness,
Just the things, which matter to you.
Let my heart be your home,
A place you freely abide,
And where sins no longer hide.

REFLECTION

Have you learnt to pray?

Who will you pray to?

How often will you pray?

What is your expectation after praying?

Do you want to experience the power of prayer?

Be inspired by prayer

Grow with prayer

Will you become a prayer warrior?

Find peace and comfort in God, through prayer

CHAPTER

POETRY

A Prayer

Father in heaven, I seek your face,
Without you, there is no saving grace.
You alone, knows my heart,
There is nothing that you cannot see,
Keep me close to you and we will never be apart.
Ever so often, I let myself strayed from your words,
But Dear Father, please restore faith in me,
That my life will align with your way, in one accord.
Holy one above, today, this is my plea,
So humble me, in your presence on my bending knees.

Hell and Back

Transported to the scene of hell,
I heard voices of the earth, screaming in torture,
It was not the gleeful sound of the Sunday morning church bell.
I stood back and watched people burning uncontrollably,
And death did not even seem near—it was pure torture,
Thank God, I could come back and share the story.
My body shivered, and my heart sunken,
Straight away, I knew, this is not a place for me,
Honestly, I much rather heaven.
Hell, is no place to go,
So people of the world, hell is real,
And that is what I want you all to know.

Devil's Kingdom

A place for the devil and his wannabe's,
I am not a part of that clan,
I am aiming for the garden of Eden, God promised me.
Hell is not a warm, cosy place,
I can tell, it really is scorching hot,
With no rescue service or saving grace.
Hell is not a place we can comprehend,
Let us stand fast in good stead,
That heaven may be our home, in the end.

The Furnace

Pitch-black and crimson red,
The torturing flame rose, as everyone hoped to be dead,
And brought this hell to an abrupt end.
But the wild flame spread through the land,
Claiming all those in its paths,
As Satan stood aside with sinners' souls, in the palm of his hands.
People cried tirelessly, until they could no more,
Yet their living bodies, endured the gruesome pain from the flames,
They wished for hope,
And worst of all, there was no way to cope.
No last chance to pray, and ask God for His forgiveness,
It was the end,
And all else faded, into the grand fiery furnace.

Meaningless

Hell will dominate the land of the unholy,
When all will be tortured with no mercy.
People will not even find their voice to speak,
All their strength will be gone, leaving them hopelessly weak.
Bodies will be rolling over each other,
Without a thought of their brothers and sisters.
As the excruciating fire will rage,
With no consideration of anyone's age.
Hell is ordained,
There are no two ways around the consequences for unrighteousness,
It will be days and years in the red-hot flames,
And the windows of heaven will be closed; hence, no rain.
All the things we gathered before the day, will be meaningless,
And the flashing point, will be righteousness!

Fear

The scorching heat of hell, left me feeling fearful,
Seen all that was great about life, suddenly disappeared,
And nothing appeared blissful.
I wanted to cry, but the tears were not coming,
It must have been the shock, of seeing bodies burning.
A scene which overwhelmed my mind, even now,
I am uneasy, just knowing if I do not get a heavenly crown,
Then, I am hell bound.

Dear Jehovah

Your love is so patient and kind,
Embed your love in my heart,
Let me be meek and gentle, like a child.
Bless my body with such strength,
That I may endure life's challenges,
And embrace situational changes.

Their Words

The words of our fore parents,
Pray to God, before you go to bed,
He has provided a comfortable place, to rest your weary head.
As you walk the road of life,
Do not ever forget faith, hope, and peace,
These are things, your heart should surely keep.
Live in love and harmony,
And stress not yourself, if there is not sufficient money,
As it will only last for a while,
And happiness is for a lifetime.

I Look to Thee

Lift me up, oh Lord,
For my face is towards the ground,
Let my eyes, see the light,
And my heart and soul sing your praises, in one accord.
Give me strength, to speak thy words,
As they are my only swords.
Let me remember these days,
When your mercies, unto me, you gave.
Oh God, lift me up on high,
As I look to you, in the bright blue skies.

God's Guidance

I pray for guidance and strength each day,
Lest, I rely on my own will and go astray.
Teach me Father, to be kind,
Because it is your will and not mine.
Please let me continuously seek thy face,
It is the only place, I find saving grace.
I pray you dwell, more in me,
Dear Lord, as I pray these simple words to Thee.

Let Me Listen . . .

Let me learn to listen to your still voice,
This I know, will take me through the darkest night,
Let me hear your voice, oh Lord . . .
As words spoken, will be my light . . .

In God's Love

Let me find myself in you,
That I may be holy too.
Let your blessings flow through me,
And all the things, I may do to please Thee.
Let my kindness, touch the hearts of many,
And your work, I will continue to do beautifully.

Forgiveness

Please forgive me, Father,
For the mountain of things, I have done wrong,
I hate to go about, with my sins laid on me like a log.
Take my burden, let me be light as feathers,
Teach me how to fly with you,
So my heart may be in sync with you forever.

Forgive Others

Learn to forgive each other,
Not just your sister or your brother,
But everyone, as all belong to our father.
Your heart is unfathomable,
Capable of holding all the things, that make you comfortable.
Hesitate not, to make room for love,
Or your heart will be plagued with savagery,
It is much better with great things, that would not let you worry.
Fill it with contentment and joyfulness,
Even some warmth and a little kindness.

Heart

Touch my heart with your miracle hands,
Let me only desire the things which are true,
That I may lead a life that is good,
With strong hope of seeing the promised land.

Father, I Am Here

Before your throne, I bow down,
Submitting all I am, at your feet,
Simplifying my ways in your holy presence, as your own.
Strip me daily of my sinful ways,
And let the words of my mouth, match those in my heart,
That my tongue may speak holiness,
And not be swayed to slay.
Open my eyes to see your will,
And my faith will grow in Thee.

Joyful Noise unto the Lord

I will sing you praises, all day long,
I will sing the sweetest words, from my favourite songs.
I will let my heart rejoice, in the beauty of your love,
Because, Dear Lord, you are my Heavenly Dove.

Great God

I want the world to know, how great you are,
My God, you are my Supreme,
My ever-shining guiding star.
So I will shout it out aloud,
Until your praises are heard, through the bright white clouds.

Christian Mind

A Christlike mind, is my aspiration,
No lies, fights or adulteration.
The praying type, I want to be,
To commit myself to formal prayer, kneeling on my knees.
I know, a Christian mind should be about purity,
And not only about praying,
So I aim to do my best, day out and day in.

CHAPTER

LETTER TO MY LOVED ONES

Dear Loved Ones,

I am writing to say thank you for all your time and support. I am tremendously blessed to have you in my life, and I trust life will continue to be kind to us all. As you are now aware of my spiritual experiences of hell, I am also trusting we are getting our lives in order. It is so easy to endure a sinful life, with little or no thought and regard for our Father in heaven. But when things appear easy, with little or no cost, that is when I am more likely to question where I am at with my spiritual life. So I am hoping that at the end of this life, we will be in heaven together, rejoicing with God and His angels. I sincerely hope heaven—the promised land, the most beautiful garden we will ever see—will be ours forever! I can only imagine the joy in our hearts should we make it there. A beautiful new place awaits us—let it be my darlings, let it be.

Let us continue to do what we really must, to make it through the pearly gates of heaven. What a day? What a day this would be? According to that old-time song we all know quite well. I am hoping you remember this one too: 'My home is heaven, just waiting for me, and when I reach there how happy I will be . . . ' I would hate nothing more than for us to be searching for each other.

Life has a way of throwing us to the walls sometimes, but we must never give up. We ought to continue seeking strength through faith and prayer. 1 Thessalonians 5:16 encourages us to pray without ceasing. And Mark 11:22 reminds us, Jesus told His people to have faith in God! Therefore, let us continue to do the good work of faith in God's honour. James 2:26 says, 'Faith without works is dead.'

My dear ones, I just truly hope we will continue to absorb and breathe the word of God Almighty. May our lives forever shine like the stars above, as we continue this wonderful spiritual journey. Keep your eyes firmly on the heavenly prize, as there is nothing to lose.

For My Family

Dear God, thank you for my family,
And for allowing us to pray and stay together,
Without them, I would struggle a lot.
You made them wonderfully special,
And I am entirely grateful.
You taught us the importance of faith and prayer,
And they never ceased to unlock our blessings.
Almighty Father, thank you for the greatness family brings.
You are amazing, super amazing.

CHAPTER

THOUGHTS

PLAN OF ACTION

TODAY:

TOMORROW:

SHORT TERM:

LONG TERM:

PERMANENT:

NO TURNING BACK:

PRAYER PLAN

_____

_____

_____

_____

_____

_____

_____

_____

_____

_____

_____

_____

_____

_____

_____

_____

_____

_____

_____

_____

_____

_____

_____

_____

_____

REPENT

Respond to the word of God

Every day, and shed your sins

Place your faith in the one true God, Jehovah, and

Encourage others to accept Christ and

Not the Devil

Today is your day, so make a start before it is too late

HELL IS REAL . . .

READ THE BIBLE!

DO NOT BE CLUELESS!

DO NOT BE LOST!

DO NOT BE FOOLED BY THE DEVIL AND HIS FALSE WORKERS!

DO NOT SLUMBER AND SLEEP . . .

WAKE UP AND SMELL HEAVEN, NOT THE COFFEE AND
DEFINITELY NOT HELL!

LET YOUR LIFE SHINE FOR GOD

LET YOUR LIGHT SO SHINE BEFORE MEN, THAT THEY MAY SEE YOUR GOOD WORKS, AND GLORIFY YOUR FATHER WHICH IS IN HEAVEN (MATT. 5:16).

KEEP THE PRAYER LINE OPEN. GOD IS ALWAYS THERE WAITING FOR THAT SPECIAL CONNECTION.

FOR THE EYES OF THE LORD ARE ON THE RIGHTEOUS AND HIS EARS ARE ATTENTIVE TO THEIR PRAYER, BUT THE FACE OF THE LORD IS AGAINST THOSE WHO DO EVIL (1 PET. 3:12).

PRAYER GIVES CONFIDENCE

AND THIS IS THE CONFIDENCE THAT WE HAVE IN HIM, THAT, IF WE ASK ANYTHING ACCORDING TO HIS WILL, HE HEARETH US (1 JOHN 5:14).

GOD ONLY ASKED FOR US TO DO ONE THING . . .

THIS IS A FAITHFUL SAYING, AND THESE THINGS I WILL THAT THOU AFFIRM CONSTANTLY, THAT THEY WHICH BELIEVED IN GOD MIGHT BE CAREFUL TO MAINTAIN GOOD WORKS. THESE THINGS ARE GOOD AND PROFITABLE UNTO MEN (TITUS 3:8).

IF YOU HAVE ONE THING TO GIVE, MAKE IT YOUR SOUL, AND GIVE IT TO JESUS!

JESUS SAID UNTO HIM, THOU SHALT LOVE THE LORD THY GOD WITH ALL THY HEART, AND WITH ALL THY SOUL, AND WITH ALL THY MIND (MATT. 22:37).

CHOOSE HEAVEN AND MAKE IT YOUR HOME!

THESE THINGS I HAVE WRITTEN UNTO YOU THAT BELIEVE ON THE NAME OF THE SON OF GOD; THAT YE MAY KNOW THAT YE HAVE ETERNAL LIFE, AND THAT YE MAY BELIEVE ON THE NAME OF THE SON OF GOD (1 JOHN 5:13).

INDEX

CPSIA information can be obtained
at www.ICGtesting.com
Printed in the USA
BVHW070439090421
604501BV00008B/1105